How to Fin

7 Easy Steps to Master Job Searching, Job Hunting, Job Offer Application Planner & Job Seeking

Theodore Kingsley

More by Theodore Kingsley

Discover all books from the Career Development Series by Theodore Kingsley at:

bit.ly/theodore-kingsley

Book 1: How to Write a Resume

Book 2: How to Write a Cover Letter

Book 3: How to Find a Job

Book 4: How to Prepare for Job Interviews

Book 5: How to Brand Yourself

Book 6: How to Network

Book 7: How to Develop Your Career

Book 8: How to Change Careers

Themed book bundles available at discounted prices:

bit.ly/theodore-kingsley

Copyright

Under no circumstances will any legal responsibility or blame be held against the publisher for any reparation, damages, or monetary loss due to the information herein, either directly or indirectly.

Respective authors own all copyrights not held by the publisher.

The information herein is offered for informational purposes solely, and is universal as so. The presentation of the information is without contract or any type of guaranteed assurance.

The trademarks that are used are without any consent, and the publication of the trademark is without permission or backing by the trademark owner. All trademarks and brands within this book are for clarifying purposes only and are the owned by the owners themselves, not affiliated with this document.

Table of Contents

Introduction

Welcome to How to Find a Job. So, you're applying for jobs. No one really wants to be there—it is a frightening thing to put yourself out there. You are putting your professional history all in front of you to be scrutinized in under ten seconds. Did you know that the average hiring manager only spends about six seconds on a resume to determine whether it is going to make it into the interview pile or not? This means that you have just six seconds to make your resume stand out enough to get a callback.

Intimidated?

Most people are. It is a daunting thing to be in that position of being judged when your judge, jury, and executioner will only take six seconds to disregard your application, only to never call you and leave you wondering what went wrong. If you'd like to avoid that, however, this guide is here to help you.

We all need money to live, and that means that for all but the independently wealthy, those born into wealth, and those who are just plain lucky, will have to work at some point or another, and that means applying for jobs. Whether you are applying for your first job or you are applying to a new position, this guide is here to help you.

We will be discussing how you can get a job, condensing it all down to just 7 easy steps. If you are ready to get started with work and you know that this is something that you are determined to do, then keep following the guide... You will be able to brush up your job application skills in no time, and you will find yourself being capable of great things—all by being well aware of what it will take. While it is, in theory, as simple as applying for a job and calling it good, there are other considerations to make that will dramatically up your chances of getting that job that you are looking for. Whether it is a side-grade or an upgrade in terms of pay, you can get it.

Let's get started!

Chapter 1: Step 1 - Consider Your Skillset

So, you have decided that you want a new job, or it could be your first job ever. It is time for you to get started—so what do you do first? You could go straight to Craigslist and start applying willy-nilly to every single job that even remotely sounds interesting without reading any of the requirements or considering how you would feel about it. You could choose to put in random applications to jobs. However, this is not going to be the most effective use of your time or energy. You could do this—but you could also choose to make use of one simple step that will change the course of your life forever—or at the very least, help you avoid wasting time during your application process. No, don't just apply to it all and hope something will stick. You need to be strategic about your applications. You need to think it through and know exactly what you are doing at all points in time.

How do you do this, you may ask?

Simple: You consider your skillset.

Yes, this one little step can actually dramatically change your job search for the better. This one step can guide you so that you look primarily at jobs that are worth it. You will be applying primarily for jobs that you will be able to profit from and jobs that will be suited to your own personal skills. By paying attention to your skillset, in particular, you know that you are giving yourself that direct consideration that you need—you are helping yourself to remain focused, so you do not waste time on jobs that are irrelevant or barely relevant to you.

What Is a Skillset?

Of course, you may be wondering what a skillset is. You can't consider your skillsets if you don't know what skill sets are, of course. Thankfully, they are quite simple to understand. Your skillet is sort of the culmination of who you are and what you are. It combines your knowledge, your own personality, and the skills that you have developed over the course of your life into nice packages that you can usually summarize in just a few words.

Skillsets primarily come in two forms: soft skills and hard skills. Each of these will provide you with a different insight into the kind of person that you are. Soft skills are those relevant to your ability to get along with other people. They are your interpersonal skills, and while important, they are typically quite difficult to gauge if you are not in an interview with someone. This is often referred to as emotional intelligence—the way that you can understand, empathize, and listen to other people, among other things. This skillset focuses on how well you can interact in social settings and is directly relevant to your job search because people skills go far. If you want to be successful, you must have good people skills to back you up.

Hard skills, on the other hand, are quantifiable. These are skills that you are taught or that you develop over time. This is your technical know-how or your ability list or experience that you have that qualify you for a job. For example, you might have a hard skill in programming computers or speaking Spanish. You might also have a hard skill of working on computers, training dogs, or even being a doctor. These skills matter and are closely related to whatever field that you will be applying to. While your social skills will matter in all jobs, your hard skills are what will set you apart from other applicants.

Both soft and hard skills will matter in your job search. However, hard skills will be evaluated first. This is why you need your hard skills considered, honed, and expressed during your job search—they will be your first line of defense against those six seconds before your resume ends up in the trash. The soft skills come into play later—this will help to differentiate between two people who have the same qualifications. Typically, the one with the better people skills will win out over the one that is a bit more awkward, even if the awkward one has slightly better qualifications.

What Are Your Skillsets?

Of course, this means that you must figure out your own skillsets. Trying to figure out your own will require you to consider your own personal strengths. What do you do well? What do you struggle with? Figure out what you do well and make sure that you apply it to what you are doing. Let's go over a few of the most common skillsets based on careers:

Administrative Career Skillsets

When you work administrative careers, you usually work to run an office or business, taking care of the paperwork or other information that must be done to keep everything running. The skills that you will need for this range from being able to utilize software to run an office to being capable of coordinating between departments with ease and more. Some common skills include:

- Collaboration
- Communication (Written and verbal)
- Coordinating events
- Critical thinking
- Interpersonal skills
- Managing documents
- Managing job-specific software
- Managing time well
- Organization
- Problem-solving
- Strong customer service skills
- Working with Microsoft Office

Sales Career Skillsets

When you work in sales, you are in a difficult spot in which you must be able to sell while also being able to communicate well with others. You must be able to mix several skillsets together to succeed in sales, such as:

- Active listening
- Branding
- Client acquisition and retention
- Collaboration
- Customer relationship management
- Emotional intelligence
- Managing a project
- Managing a team
- Managing accounts
- Negotiation
- Networking
- Persuasion
- Public speaking

Education Career Skillsets

Education is a difficult career path but is also incredibly rewarding for those who get into it. You may require a certain degree of skillsets. If you want to get into an education career, you want skills such as:

- Active listening
- Assessment skills
- Classroom management
- Collaboration
- Communication (written and verbal)
- Computer skills
- Flexibility
- Instructional skills
- Interpersonal skills
- Leadership
- Organization
- Public speaking skills
- Time management

Information Technology Skillsets

If you want to work in IT, you will require a certain degree of hard and soft skills combined. There are many different facts to IT so what those around you want may vary significantly. However, you can expect to see these skills in the desired list:

- Analytics
- Cloud computing
- Collaboration
- Communicating complex information simply
- Critical thinking

- Cybersecurity
- IP setup
- JavaScript
- Multitasking
- Networking
- Project management
- Python
- Wireless modems/routers
- Written and verbal communication

No matter what career you choose to pursue, you will need to understand what it will take for you to succeed. You must be willing and able to see the different skills that you can get in with ease, and that takes time and effort. However, if you can get it right, you can actually make great progress. You can actually start to get those callbacks that you are looking for, and all you will need to do is make sure that you actually record the right skillsets.

This is precisely why it is so important for you to take the time to tailor your resume and cover letter to each type of job that you are applying for. Someone who wants an IT job will have a very different focus than someone wishing to apply to a teaching job or a customer service job. The jobs are so different that you will see that there are also different types of responses to them. You must make sure that you always put out the right skills if you want your resume to actually catch the eye of your hiring manager and that hiring managers will almost always be prioritizing the skills that are relevant to their particular field.

If you desire a job in a field that was not listed here, and there are several out there, then do some research. Consider what you would need to do to get those better-paying jobs. Make sure that you know what it is that the field that you are interested in cares about. If you can identify that, you can figure out exactly what you should be doing.

Developing Your Skillsets

If you intend to get into a new career but find that you do not yet have the skillset, don't worry—you can work to develop the right one as well. Some skills will require formal training, and the jobs that require this will be very stringent about this. They will tell you that they require certain certifications and that you must prove it. This is the case for, for example, doctors to practice medicine. Certain jobs are simply so complex that you will need formal training. Others will allow for more flexibility. If you do not have the education necessary for your dream job, then you will need to find it somewhere along the way.

When it comes to simply figure out your skillsets, however, you have some other options available to you as well. If you want to determine your skillsets so you can begin to develop them, consider the following:

What Do You Enjoy Doing?

Tasks that you enjoy that you are also competent in are usually a good starting point for you. Maybe you've found that there are certain skills that simply make you feel more invested in what you are doing, or you feel particularly good when you go through them. It does not have to come naturally or easily to you—but you should enjoy it. This will help you figure out the right kinds of jobs for you as well—if you find that you enjoy working with numbers and trying to solve problems, you would probably be suited to certain financial type positions, but if you find that you actually prefer to work with people, you may be a better teacher or customer service representative.

Consider What People Compliment

When you receive compliments at work, what are you doing at that point in time? What is it that you do that will get those good comments from other people? You might realize through a bit of reflection that you are commonly praised for thinking outside of the box or for figuring out why the printer kept jamming when you'd try to print out papers. This is a great indicator of where you should look for your skillsets. People compliment things that you are good at, and if you are good at something, you shouldn't let those skills go to waste.

Consider the Different Jobs You've Worked

Stop and think about all of the different jobs that you have worked, even if they seemed unrelated to the jobs that you think that you might like to work in the future. You want to consider those different jobs that you have worked and think about what skills you developed during the course of that time. What did you do that helped you? How did you learn what you needed to do? What was it that helped you? When you figure this out, you can better come up with a running master list of your skillsets that you can draw from as necessary for the various applications you submit.

Chapter 2: Step 2 - Updating and Preparing Your Resume

Your resume is the first point of contact between yourself and the other person. It is through the resume that hiring managers start to figure out what to expect. Your resume has to be good if you want to get hired, and that means you need to know exactly what you must put on it. Due to the fact that you know that managers will not be spending ample time reading through your resume, you want to make it stand out, send the message that it is supposed to send in as few words as possible in ways that will actively draw the attention of the hiring manager. Your resume must be clear, concise, and put your best foot forward. If you cannot do that, you are going to struggle to get that job that you were looking for.

In this chapter, we will go over four key steps that you should take for your resume. Now, if you don't know how to write a resume, there are dozens of generators that you can use online that will help you to get your resume all organized and lined up exactly as they should be. They will simply fill in blanks on a template with information that you provide, which you can then utilize as your own resume. Generally speaking, that should be good enough for your resume for most jobs.

What Goes on a Resume?

Before you begin, you must ensure that you have all of the right information on your resume. If you leave anything major out on your resume, you run the risk of causing problems for yourself. You will need to keep your resume lined up properly if you want to get those job callbacks, and that means that you need to know what to provide. Keep in mind that the best resumes are condensed down as much as possible, preferably on one page, so the manager can see everything without having to flip through pages. Let's go over the primary sections of any well-prepared resume:

Contact Information

Your resume will begin with contact information. This is crucial—you must have contact information if you want the hiring manager to call you back. This should be at the very top of your resume is easily read font. Additionally, you want to make sure that all contact information is accurate. If you have recently changed your phone number, it's time to update it. In particular, you should expect to provide information such as:

- Name and address (updated)
- Email address (must be professional, and preferably utilizing your name)
- Phone numbers (must be updated and make sure that you check your voicemail prompt to ensure there is nothing unprofessional there

- Online portfolios (if relevant)

Objective Statement

After your contact information is completed, you may use an objective statement. This is something that may not be present on every single resume that you create, but it can be a highly beneficial inclusion, depending upon the job you are aiming for. Remember that your objective should always be clear; it should define exactly what you want to do and be tailored to whatever you are applying to. If not in your resume, then it should be included in your cover letter.

Summary Statement

You may also consider using a summary statement. This is meant to highlight why you should be hired in just four or five lines of text. This is commonly used in lieu of an objective statement and is most commonly the part of your resume that is read. It should summarize your skills, achievements, and experience in just a couple of brief sentences. Make sure to use keywords when making your summary statement and ensure that you tailor this to every single job you apply to—no two employers should get the same summary statement.

Employment History

When applying for work, you must also provide your employment history. This is one of the best ways that you will be able to present work experience and, therefore, skills that you have. If you want to do this, you must do so in a way that makes sense. Most of the time, this is chronological, and most people will assume that you do so as well. This means that you must start with your current job and then work backward. Include the job title, employer, location of the employment, and the time frame that you have worked at that position. Then, you must add a summary of what you did.

Education

Of course, you want to highlight your education. You should always start with your highest degree or the most recent degree if you went back to school and the new degree is more relevant to the job that you are applying to. Ensure that you include the name and location of the school, as well as which degree you have received and the major.

Other Information

Finally, you will include any other information that may not fit into any of the earlier categories but objectively would help you get a better job or be a better fit for what you wish to apply for. For example, you may try to include your memberships to organizations, work done voluntarily, skills that you have, or awards received. Generally speaking, however, you want to avoid religion or politics here unless directly relevant to the job that you are applying for.

Keep in mind that you will not include references on your resume. We will talk more about this later in the guide, but remember to leave them off of your resume. Remember, you will be assumed to be capable of providing them.

Respond to the Job Application

When you sit down to apply for jobs, you must make sure that you don't make the mistake of just printing out a one-size-fits-all resume and sending it off to every single place of employment on that list that you have. This is a surefire way to get many of them thrown out entirely. If you want to attract the attention of the hiring manager, you must ensure that you apply the right way. You need to ensure that you are responding to your job applications. Your resume should focus on what they are asking for—make sure that you are using keywords that make it clear that you have read the resume. You should ensure that your resume highlights each and every point that they are asking for. You want to make sure that you are responding directly to their individual application, even if that means that you have to stop and rewrite it each time.

Describe and Focus on Accomplishments (Not Responsibilities)

When you are crafting your resume, you might struggle to write up what you did at each job you had. After all, how many ways can you say that you worked an office job? How many ways can you phrase things so they can stand out? Imagine that you were a cashier, and you want to write about it. You would need to find a way to express what you have done. The gut reaction is often phrasing things, so you list out your responsibilities. However, that requires you to use mostly passive language instead of active. If you want to ensure that the resume stands out, you want active, powerful language, and you get that through describing your accomplishments.

Instead of, for example, saying that you have kept things organized at work, you would want to state that you have optimized the turnaround time in what you were doing. Or, instead of saying that you provided customer service, you could state that you were working to provide expert customer retention work, with an 85% retention rate. By focusing on what you have achieved instead of what you were responsible for, your resume will be more powerful by making sure that you do this, you up to your chances of getting noticed.

Emphasizing Transferable Skills

If you are writing your resume for the first time and have followed the earlier information, then it is time to start considering how to make your resume stand out above the rest. If you want your resume to make it into the contact pile, then don't make a bland resume. You must make sure that when you create it, you really sell yourself. This is not the time to let modesty win. After all, remember—if you do not hook the hiring manager within just a few seconds, you will not hear back from them.

One way to help your resume become something memorable is to emphasize your transferable skills. These are the skills that you have built up over the course of your time of employment at certain jobs that can then directly be applied to the new job that you are attempting to apply for. These skills are highly beneficial and show that you are capable of the work. For example, imagine a hairstylist applying for work as a dental assistant. At first glance, they are not similar at all, but the truth is, they share many similarities. Both hairstylists and hygienists will have to mix together materials—with stylists mixing dyes and hygienists combining the cleaning materials they will need. This is important to keep in mind—it might not be the same job, but the skills still hold. That individual knows that they can follow directions and mix things together without a problem.

When you create your summary statement, make sure that you work hard to really emphasize those transferable skills to the best of your ability. This is precisely how you stick out and get those callbacks.

Focus on Abilities

Next, when it comes to working on your resume, you want to make sure that you focus on your abilities. When you write your resume, your hobbies often do not matter unless they are directly relevant to your job, and in some instances, they may be. Someone who loves video gaming, for example, may list that it is a hobby of theirs on their application. But, for the most part, you do want to focus on abilities. What are your skills? Do you have any awards or accolades to back it up? Think about this—you want to make sure that the other person who is reading your resume knows that you have these marketable skills and knows that you are going to utilize them in some way or another. You want them to know this, so they feel more interested in you as an applicant.

When you feel yourself shifting over to talking about hobbies on your resume, try to turn it around into skills. You might be good at playing video games—may be that is due to being highly perceptive, capable of responding rapidly, or something similar. If your hobby is baking, maybe you emphasize the skill of following directions effectively and being able to understand them quickly. No matter what your hobbies are, find a way to turn them around so you can use the abilities for your hobby to your advantage.

Ensure Social Media Matches the Resume

Finally, when it comes to lining up your resume, do not forget that we are in the era of digital information and social media. If you have any social media, make sure that it is all cleaned up now—you do not want to try to apply for a job if you have unsavory material on your social media. Likewise, you want to ensure that LinkedIn, if you use it, is filled out properly as well. You want to ensure that the information provided on your resume is also directly reflected on LinkedIn just due to the fact that people will double-check it.

Going through your social media can help you to ensure that your entire resume is as clean as possible to get you the best possible chance at success that you can get. If you want to land a job, you must be able to create a resume to show that you are worth it.

Chapter 3: Step 3 - Consider the Kinds of Companies You Wish to Work For

The next step to consider when it comes to finding a new job is figuring out where it is that you want to work in the first place. You should be able to figure out what kinds of companies that you would prefer to work for. What kinds of companies are right for you? Do you want to find a job that involves working at a big corporation? Or would you prefer to work somewhere smaller? Do you want a job working in an admin situation or something else?

Within this chapter, we are going to take a look at how to start considering the right kind of company that will help you to achieve exactly what you were looking for. Choosing good job matters. You need to know that you are at a company that you can trust and which will respect you and ensure that at the end of the day, you feel content and comfortable. Knowing that you can trust where you are is highly important—it helps you to ensure that you know precisely what you will need. When you work on your consideration of which kinds of companies you would prefer, there are a few key considerations that will help you to figure out how to narrow it down. The truth is, what is right for you may not be right for other people, and you will need to figure out what works for everyone involved. IF you want to ensure that you are on the right track, you must start by figuring out the considerations that you will make. Let's go over the key considerations now.

Consider Staff Turnover

First, let's consider the turnover rate at various companies. When you are looking at a company and trying to figure out its worthiness for you to apply, one of the best starting points is to ask about the staff turnover. This will tell you a lot about how the people that work there are valued. You will need to consider the fact that there are various people in various positions, and all of those positions will determine what you see quite well. Figure out what the current staff turnover rate is. If it is high, you have to wonder why people are so eager to leave the job in the first place. If it is low, you may see that the place takes care of its employees or that employees simply love to work there. There is probably a good reason for it. If you see that turnover is low, people probably want to settle there, and that means that you should have all sorts of reasons to want to stick to it if at all possible.

Consider Company Performance

Next, consider company performance. Think about what it means to have a healthy company, first of all, because you want to work somewhere that you are confident is going to have everything that you will need to get started. Being able to see how the company is performing helps you to understand if your company will remain around if you do choose it. If your company were to go under, you would be out of a job, and understandably, most people would prefer to avoid this if at all possible.

Consider Work-Life Balance

You will also want to think about what it is that they want from you. Just how much work do they really want you to do? Can you keep up with it? Can you ensure that you will actually be able to take care of everything if you are following that work-life balance? Will you be happy? Of course, we all have our own work-life balances that we are willing to tolerate. We all have different degrees of comfort that we are willing to expose ourselves to and that means that you will also need to make sure that ultimately, whatever it is that you have chosen to do will be tolerable for you. Will you be forced to work far more than you can deal with? Will your job encroach on precious family time? If so, you may have a serious problem that you will need to address somehow. Figure out what you can do to address those issues. If the job will simply demand too much from you and you are not interested in following through, then you will need to find a job that you can tolerate. If you are unhappy with the work-life balance, your work time will be miserable. Make sure that you find something that you genuinely enjoy, so you know that you are in a position that you can do well. If you have a family that you want to be home for every single night, make sure that you don't pick a job that would require, for example, you to take care of business trips.

Consider Company Culture

Company culture is another major consideration that you will need to make. Are you someone who is going to naturally fit in with the people around you? Will you be able to fit in without feeling uncomfortable? Sometimes, company culture is the determining factor for why someone else gets fired, especially in at-will states where people can be filed for literally any reason. If you want to ensure that you can make it work in any company that you will work, you must make sure that the company culture matches. For example, if you are ultra-conservative, you probably would not feel very at home working in a very liberal environment. Likewise, if you were of a certain religion and felt that religion was not honored where you are considering working, you would probably feel uncomfortable as well. You need to make sure that you are somewhere that you are able to find that comfort with others. When you choose the right company for you, you will fit in seamlessly with the culture around you, and that is how you know that you are in the right spot. It is imperative that you are in that position so that you can feel at home with the people around you.

Consider What the Company Offers You

You should also figure out if the company that you are looking at will actually offer you something of value. You should see if there is any way to take advantage of that opportunity that you are looking for. If you can do so, you should say yes and take advantage of it. If not, however, you should probably find a way to verify that you actually enjoy what you are being offered. Do you enjoy the company that you would potentially be working for? Do you think that you would get something back if you did something for them? Do you feel like they will provide you with something that will help you to progress your career?

Career progression is not necessarily a new job or bigger responsibilities—it can also be developing your skills and becoming more adept in your own professional field. If a company has no room for growth, it is probably not a very good one to enter if you are trying to advance your career. You will need to ensure that you can and will be able to work toward bettering yourself. Ask yourself what each of these companies offers you in terms of what they offer you to take control of and what you can gain from them. Oftentimes, the best things that you can gain are experience and learning opportunities that will help you to further your career.

Consider the Purpose You Wish to Live

Finally, consider what the purpose is for the jobs that you are looking at. Do you want to feel like you are serving a greater purpose if you were to work for any of these companies? Do you want to make sure that you feel like you are in a position of control or like you do not have to worry so much about what you do and when you do it? Though you might think that your purpose as an employee is simply to make money and to do the work, that's not it. You should also have a sense of meaning and pride in your work. Do you enjoy what you are doing? Do you love being able to figure out what it is that you are doing and completing those tasks? If so, then make sure that you can identify those things for yourself. Find the purpose of the various companies that you look at and then consider whether you want to be a part of them as well. You may find that ultimately, you can and will discover that the best purpose of all is that which will align with your own personal values.

Chapter 4: Step 4 - Start Planning and Make Your List

Job searching actually has a pretty specific method to it. If you know what you are doing, you should be able to make a streamlined approach to how you choose to find out which jobs are going to work for you. Applying for jobs takes a lot of time already—do you really want to waste more just because you didn't pay attention to the way that you should have chosen to go about your work? Most people want to take care of business as quickly as possible and streamline that attempt to find the newest career line that you are interested in. this new career could be just about anything—but you will need to know how to approach the situation.

Being able to plan out your job search is one of the best ways that you will be able to figure out how to approach what you are doing at any point in time. It all begins with understanding how to orient everything, so ultimately, what you do yields the best results. If you organize everything just right, you should be able to find the right jobs for you. Developing the plan that will help you figure out how to sort out your job-hunting abilities and ensure that you focus where the focus is needed. If you do that, you should be able to succeed.

Determine Your Career Goals

Before you can begin choosing jobs to apply to, you need to understand what your current goals and aspirations are. People don't usually think about this, and that can be a huge problem for them. They don't stop and consider what they really want and what they have to offer, and the end result is they waste their time applying to jobs that don't quite fit the right track that they need to achieve. This is a huge problem. After all, time wasted is money wasted.

Take the time at the beginning of your strategy to figure out a list of your life goals and values and use those to help you guide to whatever your decision is. You ought to have a general idea of what you want and need, and that will help you to focus primarily on jobs that should be quite satisfying for you in general. This is a wonderful way to keep your focus. Your goals could be just about anything. Maybe you want to work with people, or maybe you prefer to work in settings where you are alone all day. Maybe you want a job that will allow you to work with your hands or will allow for problem-solving. Figure out those tasks that you enjoy and make them the center of your focus.

List Your Strengths and Skills

That brings us to the next point. Once you have a list of your career goals, consider all of your experiences that you have. This is relevant here—when you know what your experience and skills are, you should be able to begin eliminating jobs that you are either overqualified or underqualified for, and that will help you immensely. If you want to be able to ensure that ultimately, you can and will be able to list out those strengths and skills, you will need to find a way to ensure that you are honest with yourself. Stop and really reflect. What do you do well? What do you struggle with? Write these down.

Then, you want to consider what your strengths are. What do you do well? Are you a problem-solver? When you figure out what your best assets are, you can really apply them when it comes to trying to make everything work for you. By ensuring that you are in a position where you should be able to exploit your strengths, you should find yourself thriving and at home in the jobs that you apply to.

Ultimately, being able to list out your experience and skills will help you keep your focus where it ought to be, and that is perfect for ensuring that you get the career paths that you will need to benefit you the most.

Brainstorm Choices

Next comes being able to brainstorm as many companies and choices as you can to figure out which jobs you want and which are going to work well for you. By taking the time to brainstorm the office options that you have, such as in the previous chapter, as we discussed, you should begin to figure out what it is that you really want to do. The brainstorming process should be as simple as figuring out which companies you want to work at and eliminating the ones that you do not care so much about.

When you take the time to figure out which companies you care the most about, you should start to figure out the right ones that you will mesh with well. This is perfect for you and ought to be a major point of consideration.

Build Your To-Do List with Job Search Activities

You must also make sure that you've got a list of all of your job search activities organized. Are there deadlines for certain jobs? Do certain jobs that you are looking at require you to do something extra? Do you need to go to some testing? What about your interviews? As you go about your job-hunting strategy, you should find yourself figuring out what it will take for you to actively apply. You should be able to figure out the best way to juggle everything and which jobs to prioritize at which points in time. This is essential if you want to make sure that you can apply without missing important dates or tasks that could cause you to lose the job entirely.

It is easier than ever these days to do this as well—you can simply put all of your information into a computer or into your phone and share the calendar across several devices so you always know what you need and where you will need it from. When you do this enough, you should find exactly what you are looking for.

Create Your Job Application Strategy

When you get through enough of the material that you start to see that you have a lot on your plate, it is time to start figuring out what your job application strategy is. You want to figure out how you want to tackle everything that you need to cover. What are you going to do to ensure that you are paying close attention to what you need? How is it that you will go about making sure that you do everything on your list? Sort through it all and figure out your strategy to ensure that all additional material is completed. Do you need to do cover letters or work samples? Figure out the plan for those and make it happen. Do you need to find a way to turn in all of your information at the same time? Maybe you tell yourself that on Monday, you will do all of your cover letters, and Tuesday, you will start building together with your work samples so that you can get everything in. Once you make it nice and easy with a clear line of when you will take care of which jobs, you should find yourself thriving. Managing everything is so much easier when you know what you are doing and how you are going to do it. Make sure that you stick to the strategy, and suddenly the entire process of job applications will be so much easier.

Organize Your List and Apply

Finally, the last part of this process is making sure that you stay organized. Ensure that you've got your list all balanced out so that you can be certain that everything is done at the right time. Organize the jobs that have been completed versus those that have not and figure out the right way to balance it all. When you do this, you should find that being able to navigate through the entire hiring process is so much easier than you thought. This is perfect for you.

Put everything into a spreadsheet with each of the different actions that you must complete as different categories. Perhaps, you have a line in your list for the application, the cover letter, the resume, work sample, and anything else that you need to submit as columns on your spreadsheet, and then you have a list of job apps in the rows. You can then manually date each cell where you have completed the corresponding job. This will help you to keep everything nice and organized, and you will be able to tell at a glance what you have done.

Chapter 5: Step 5 - Networking

Although your own skills carry with them their own merit, there is more to getting a job than simply having the right skills. You will also need to take the time to find ways to network. Networking is a critical part of your job application journey and will help you to find a way to ensure that you can and will successfully navigate through your job hunt. When you network, you effectively build up good, quality relationships with people that you can know and trust to be helpful in your journey to finding the right job for you.

The truth is, many people completely disregard the idea of needing to network with others. They don't pay attention to the fact that they need to actually get those connections to help them to be certain that they are on the right track to successfully navigate just about any situation that they find themselves in. However, in your job search, networking can help in several ways. You will be able to network to find a connection with other people. You will be able to ensure that you properly navigate the right way. You need to take the time to connect to others. If you do so the right way, you should find that your networking can help you to connect with others. You should also find that you've got the necessary job references as well.

Thankfully, networking isn't as hard as you might think. You can actually begin to develop those skills that you want or need with ease if you know what you are doing. We're going to consider a few key tips that will help you with your own networking journey now.

Do It in Person

It all begins with doing it in person. You might be tempted to network from behind your screen just because you know that doing so will help you to hide from anything that you might not want to deal with. You might be nervous, for example, so you make it a point to network through emails or chatting online. But, the problem with this is that you are not getting that same degree of connection that you need with them. You need that face-to-face interaction together to help you properly navigate through everything that you will need to do. If you want to do this the right way, that means that you need to meet up in person.

During face-to-face meetups, you can usually do so much more with your relationship. You will be able to build a personal and professional relationship if you know what you are doing, and ultimately, that's what you are really looking for here. Your relationship should be just as personal as it is professional—or more so in many ways. This is because making sure that you maintain that relationship in the right manner will help you figure out how best to navigate just about any situation.

Offer to Help the Other Person

If you want to network the right way, it begins with making sure that you offer to help the other person before you expect anything in return. This is natural- you can't just go up to someone else and demand that they do something for you. Rather, you have to make sure that you are taking the time to help them to start building up the relationship rather than allowing yourself to simply ask for what you want and move on. By taking the time to help them before you ask them to help you, you should find yourself finding the right way to start your relationship off on the right foot.

Fight off Fear

You must also consider the idea of fending off your fear before you allow it to consume you. Make sure that any fear that you feel is not given the ability to hinder you or keep you from being able to do what is right. If you are introverted, you probably already struggle with the idea of networking in the first place, but if you are smart about it, you can get past the fear and allow yourself to work against it. You can teach yourself to find a way to successfully get past the negativity and navigate through your fear.

It might not be easy at first, but learning to come back from the negativity and fend it off for yourself is imperative. However, remember that your anxiety is not the end of the world, and you can actively work against it. Remind yourself that it is not the end of the world if you are rejected and that your anxiety wants you to believe that it is a far bigger deal than you thought. Really, remembering that most people aren't interested in rejecting because they are just as interested in networking matters—when you know that you are getting along with other people, you should be able to remind yourself that things will be fine—especially since you know that most people will not make it a point to reject you if you are networking in person. It is rude, and most people are not there to discriminate and avoid other people.

Patience is a Virtue

Don't forget that relationships aren't built overnight. Strong bonds with other people take time and effort, and you will need to pay attention to how you tend to foster them. Make sure that when you are fostering your relationships with other people, you choose to talk to them over a period of time. Make sure that you give your relationships time to build over time so that you can make those connections slowly but surely. Remember that you need to be patient if you want to make those new relationships.

It also takes time to foster the right relationships as well. If you want to be certain that you are on the right track to building good relationships with others, you will need to make sure that you do so in time. Sometimes, it takes longer than you would expect to find the right person to connect to, and that's okay. You just need to be patient.

When you are patient enough, you should find yourself locating the right people for you, and over time, you will realize that being able to connect with others is sassier than you thought.

Build the Relationship Before the Resume

This brings us to the idea of what you need to focus on when it comes to your networking. Though it can be easy to focus only on what you can get from other people, you need to keep in mind that ultimately, you need to look beyond just what they will do for your career. Yes, it is important for you to build your career, but it is equally as important for you to also build up the person that you want to be. You need to make sure that you focus on the person first. You should not be so worried about what you can get from the other person that you completely forget that they are a real person with real feelings that you need to respect and consider.

Building your relationship with the other person is the primary point of this sort of association with the other person. You want to make sure that you are in a position where you can and will be able to rely on someone else. If you want to be able to rely on them, you will need to have that sort of connection with them.

Don't Forget Online Networking

Keep in mind that just because you should be focusing on networking primarily in person, you should also make sure that you use online networking as well if you need to. By making sure that you use online resources too, such as social media or other similar methods, you should be able to help focus on what you need. Being able to connect in as many ways possible is crucial if you want to be successful with networking. By being able to connect well to other people, you will have those connections that you will need.

Online, you should be able to network in all sorts of ways. You could, for example, email regularly with other people. Or you could work to connect on LinkedIn or other social networks to better connect with them. And this is another way that you can relate to others.

Reach Out

Finally, don't forget that you need to reach out to others regularly as well. When you connect well with other people on a regular basis, you should be able to build those relationships better. Reaching out on a regular basis is incredibly important if you want to build those relationships with others. Try to reach out to at least a few people every week and follow up when you can.

By following up with new connections after your first contacts, such as sending them a quick thanks or asking them a question or something that is relevant to the meeting that you had just had with them, you should be able to better connect. Remember that this follow-up should be relevant to the original connection that you had with them. However, if you play your cards right, you should find that you can connect better than ever with them.

Chapter 6: Step 6 - Identify Your References

Just about every job that you ever apply to will ask you to provide references. While they will not all follow up with that reference, you still want them to be good ones. Some jobs will ask you for a list of professional references during the interview process as well. This can be tough—if you know that your references will be contacted, you naturally want to make sure that you have the best ones possible. However, if you are uncertain about the ones that you provide, you can run into all sorts of issues. This is where being able to identify who your best references will be is the best bet for you. Being able to identify the right references for you is imperative to your job source, and because of that, you do want to make sure that you choose out the right people to put down what you need.

Who Makes a Good Reference?

When you are considering choosing a reference for your job search, it is important to understand who the right people are. There are all sorts of people who you need to leave off your reference list. It is important to not put certain people on your list, or you can end up taking your attempt to get that job. Now, let's go over everything that makes someone a good reference. There are certain people that make good references that will help you with your job search.

When it comes to choosing the right references, you will want to choose in the following order:

1. Your current managers or supervisors
2. Your previous managers or supervisors
3. Your current peers or clients
4. Your previous peers or clients
5. Personal references if you have absolutely no one else to add to your list

Keep in mind that everyone that you include is going to be someone that you can trust. If you were to choose someone who may be unwilling to speak for you or who has nothing nice to say about you, then you can have some serious problems. If you have someone who is going to say that you are no good, you will struggle. This means that if your current manager is someone who will not give you a very good reference, you should move to the next person on the list. Figuring out who will give you the best references is crucial.

Who to Leave Off the Reference List

Of course, there are also people that you should leave off of your reference list as well. It can be tempting to involve personal references or people that you believe can put in a good word for you that have not worked with you professionally, but doing so is rarely the way to go. You don't want to make a point to do this, or you can run into all sorts of issues.

Adding personal references rather than professional when professional references are requested is usually seen as a problem—mainly due to the fact that including a personal reference instead implies that you lack the professional ones. You want to leave off the personal references if at all possible. Surely, you can find other sources of references.

Keep in mind that relatives that you do not work with or for should never be on your list at all. They are not usually deemed reliable because it is clear that they are going to have your best interest at heart, and they are more likely to lie than a true third party with no connection to you.

You should also make sure that you never give a fake name and contact information that links back to a friend that is going to pretend to be someone beneficial. Most recruiters have been in the field long enough that they are able to see right through the nonsense, and getting that false reference is going to get you taken right off the list of potential hires just due to the dishonesty.

Asking Your References for Permission

Before you list anyone on your references, you need to approach them first. Specifically, go up to them and ask if they are willing to be your reference. Do so in person if possible—this will allow you to get a reading of whether they want to do so for you or not. If you can see whether they seem interested in providing a reference for you or not, you can decide whether you actually want them to be included. Someone who seems less than enthusiastic is not likely to be a good reference for you, after all, and that means that you want to get a good reading on them.

Remember that if you are going to be asking people in person, you will need to pay close attention to how they respond. You will need to make it a point to accept whatever they tell you, one way or another. If they tell you that they'd rather not, you will need to respect that for them because otherwise, you run the risk of ending up trying to get a reference that is less than stellar for you. You want to make sure that your references are those who will be enthusiastic about giving you a glowing review, not someone who simply said yes to be courteous, even though they don't really want to provide it for you.

What to Do When Covertly Seeking a New Job

If you are trying to apply for new jobs without giving notice to your current employer, you might find yourself struggling with who to put down on your reference list. Chances are, you won't be able to use your current supervisors if you are trying to keep quiet about your job search. However, if at all possible, you should try asking some of your colleagues if you have built enough of a relationship with them to be your reference. Of course, you will need to trust that they will remain silent about your job search as well. They need to know that you are trusting and relying on them and that if they are not quiet about your job search, it could have very real negative implications. You will need to find a way for you to ensure that you can ultimately figure out who to put on your list and why.

Consider explaining to your interviewer that you are trying to keep your current place of employment from knowing as well. If you explain your concerns and why you don't want them to know, you should be able to get by even if you do not have any current managers on your list without too much of a problem. Many managers and hiring recruiters are understanding and even sympathetic at times if you explain the true nature of the situation and that you simply cannot use the other person on your list.

What to Give the References You Choose

Before your references are contacted by the place of employment, you would ideally provide them with a certain degree of information that will help them to figure out who or what to do. You want to make sure that you give your references certain information so they are informed about what they can expect to be asked when they are contacted. In particular, you want to make sure that you give them a copy of the job description, as well as what you would be doing. If you do this, you allow the person who is contacted to know what to say that will actually benefit you. You want to provide them with everything that they will need to make sure that they are on the right track. You want to make sure that they play up your strengths that are relevant to what you are doing and how you can be contacted. If you play your cards right, you should find that your reference is able to give you a glowing recommendation in ways that are directly relevant to the position that you wish to get.

If you've used a reference before and plan on providing their information to another recruiter, you must remember to give them a heads up as well. You can't just add them to the list without warning them. It's rude to expect them to be on call all the time for you so you can get those references, and it could actually backfire if you do not provide the information to them as you can wind up unintentionally annoying them to the point that they don't want to provide the reference for you in the first place.

Chapter 7: Step 7 - Apply for the Jobs

Finally, it is time to get down to business. It's time to actively apply for jobs. Now that you have everything ready all in one area, and you have a list of everything that you want to use to apply, you should be ready. The job application process is an incredibly important one to keep in mind because this is your first attempt to connect to the companies that you are applying to. If your application is not perfect, you might mess up your chance to actually successfully get the job that you want in the first place, and that is a huge problem. You want to ensure that you apply for the job while putting your best foot forward. This is not the time to mess up how you fill things out, and is absolutely the time to go over everything at least twice to ensure that you've got everything the way it needs to be done.

Be Prepared

The first thing you need to do before you start applying is to make sure that you know what you are applying for in the first place. Be well aware of what you are applying for so you can be certain that you are on the right track. Recognizing everything that you will need to do and how you will need to do it matters immensely, and you want to be absolutely certain that you follow through with everything that you will need. Make sure that you actively provide yourself with all of the information that you are going to need at the very beginning. For the most part, you will need information such as:

- The last several years of job history
- The last several years of addresses
- Dates and degrees or accreditations earned
- Information about criminal background

Make sure that everything on this list is as accurate as possible— you want to fact-check everything. Don't bother with guessing—if your information does not match up with what you would see on a background check, then you could be accused of lying or being dishonest about something. That can be a major problem, and if you do so, you could end up finding that you are in a position in which you are unable to get the job that you wanted. If you can't quite remember the right dates, go through your records to verify them.

Read ALL Instructions Before Beginning

Before you start applying for the job, make sure that you read all instructions. Do they want the application filled out with a pen? Through typing? Do they want you to include information on a separate sheet? Will you need to provide references to the application? Or do you need a cover letter? Make sure you're well aware of everything on the list before you begin so you can be certain that you have everything done the right way before you begin.

If you do not read all of the instructions and end up filling out the application incorrectly, you stand a very good chance of having your application thrown away just due to the fact that it is wrong. You must make sure that your application is properly filled out to avoid this from becoming a problem. Make sure you've looked through the entire application before you start filling it out as well to make sure that you do not end up duplicating information that doesn't need to be doubled.

Be as Neat as Possible

It should go without saying that your application should be filled out as neatly as possible. If you have to fill out a physical piece of paper, make sure that you take your time to make your handwriting as neat as possible and make sure that you don't scratch bits out. If you make a mistake, you will need to use correction fluid. Scribbling out as an attempt to clear out the information that is incorrect looks bad and disorganized, and that can be a huge problem. When you do this the right way, you should be able to successfully get through what you need to be done.

Neatness goes a long way. If at all possible, try to type in the information into your application. If you are able to utilize editing software to fill in a PDF copy of the application, it will look much cleaner and more professional than if you use a pencil. If you have to fill it out by hand, use pens in formal colors—blue or black only. This is not the time to test out your new purple pen or to use glow-in-the-dark ink or something else that might seem really cool in theory but is unprofessional.

You will also want to make sure that if you are turning in a physical document, it is kept as neatly as possible. This means avoiding spilling coffee on it, letting it get wrinkled up or damaged in the rain. Certainly, avoid folding it down into something small—you can end up causing yourself more problems if you do so. When you make sure that you keep your file neat, you show professionalism. You might want to consider keeping it in a folder when you are transporting it just to keep it from being bent up or damaged as you transport it to where it needs to go.

Be Honest

Make sure that everything on your application is as truthful as possible. No lying here—lying is entirely unacceptable. Yes, this even means saying that you have a GED or a high school diploma if you really don't. This is a common lie that is told, but you can get in serious trouble if you lie about it and then cannot verify it later on. Depending upon the job, you could even be fired if you lie about something only to find that it was entirely inaccurate.

Make sure that you never make up an answer on the spot, either. You cannot do this, and doing so is going to put you at more risk than anything else. By being at risk in this manner, you can run into all sorts of issues. Instead, make it a point to simply answer your questions as honestly as possible, even if the answer may be something that is not desirable.

Be Thorough

You want to make sure that all of your answers are as thorough as possible. This means that in some cases, you may have to go around to do some extra research if necessary. If you do this the right way, your application should be appealing. You need to make your answers as good as possible if you have the best chance of getting called back.

Focus on What You Offer

As you fill everything out, you might find that you find yourself wanting to list out what you do. However, instead of doing it this way, discuss your successes and your responsibilities. This is a small shift in how you apply that can actually make a huge difference in how your application is interpreted. This means making sure that you write down that your current job has you responsible for, for example, ensuring that the books are balanced at the end of the day. Instead of stating, "I budget and take care of money," you could say, "I am responsible for ensuring that the books are balanced." This shift matters.

And, if you've had a period of time where you are unemployed, you can show that you have done other things as well that would be relevant. It could be as simple as stating that you "managed a household" or stating that you have been going to school or volunteering for certain organizations. These still show dedication and that you have not just been sitting around doing nothing for all these years.

Be Concise and Clear

As you write, try to be as clear and concise as you can. This means cutting out the extra words if they aren't absolutely necessary. Try to state everything in as few words as possible. Unless you are applying for a writer's job, this is not the time to show off your flowery language—it is the time to get to the point and to avoid wasting their time. By avoiding wasting their time, you up the chances of them being able to see everything on your application. After all, most recruiters don't want to hear your whole life story—they just want to know what is relevant in as few words as possible.

Double- and Triple-Check for Errors

Finally, make sure that you cut out any errors. Before you submit your document, you should double- and triple-check it. And, if at all possible, have a fresh set of eyes look over it as well before you apply. If you don't have anyone who could proofread it, consider setting it aside for the night and coming back the next morning to see if anything stands out to you. You might find that there were some simple mistakes that would be easy to correct right there in your face for you to handle.

Conclusion

And that brings us to the end of this guide! If you've been following along, you've officially done the hardest part of everything—applying for that job that you really want! If all goes well, your next step is going to be to nail your interview. Thankfully, there are all sorts of great ways that you can make that happen. If you know what you are doing, you should find that you can prepare for that job interview with ease: You just have to know what to expect!

Now, remember—the most important point is to remember that you need to sell yourself. You are working to show the world that you are valuable and that through that value that you have to offer to everyone, you can thrive in your capabilities. Ultimately, the ability that you have to succeed will be one of the most important, and if you play your cards right, you should be able to do so.

So now, get out there! Start working on that job hunt! Put the skills you've just learned to the test, and you should have the job applications start pouring in in no time—all you have to do is begin somewhere. Good luck out there! You can absolutely get this to work for you, too! Get out there and get started!

More by Theodore Kingsley

Discover all books from the Career Development Series by
Theodore Kingsley at:

bit.ly/theodore-kingsley

Book 1: How to Write a Resume

Book 2: How to Write a Cover Letter

Book 3: How to Find a Job

Book 4: How to Prepare for Job Interviews

Book 5: How to Brand Yourself

Book 6: How to Network

Book 7: How to Develop Your Career

Book 8: How to Change Careers

Themed book bundles available at discounted prices:

bit.ly/theodore-kingsley

Printed in July 2023
by Rotomail Italia S.p.A., Vignate (MI) - Italy